The Library of Explorers and Exploration

FERDINAND MAGELLAN

The First Voyage Around the World

Betty Burnett, Ph.D.

the rosen publishing group's
rosen
central

To Melody

Published in 2003 by The Rosen Publishing Group, Inc.
29 East 21st Street, New York, NY 10010

First Edition

Library of Congress Cataloging-in-Publication Data

Burnett, Betty, 1940–
Ferdinand Magellan: the first voyage around the world / By Betty Burnett. — 1st ed.
    p. cm. — (The library of explorers and exploration)
Summary: A description of the life and voyage of the sixteenth-century Portuguese sea captain who commanded the first expedition to sail around the world.
Includes bibliographical references (p.   ).
ISBN 0-8239-3617-1 (lib. bdg.)
1. Magalhães, Fernão de, d. 1521—Juvenile literature. 2. Explorers—Portugal—Biography—Juvenile literature. 3. Voyages around the world—Juvenile literature. [1. Magellan, Ferdinand, d. 1521. 2. Explorers.
3. Voyages around the world.]
I. Title. II. Series.
G286.M2 B89 2003
910'.92—dc21

                                                                2001008533

Manufactured in the United States of America

CONTENTS

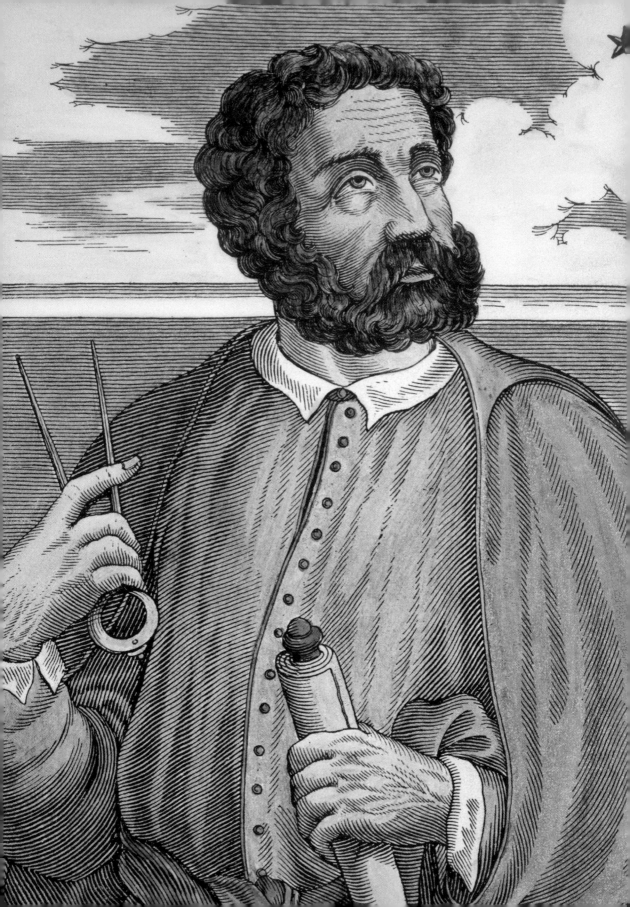

INTRODUCTION

THE GREAT AGE OF DISCOVERY

Ferdinand Magellan was born right in the middle of Europe's great age of discovery. The years between 1415 and 1578 saw hundreds of expeditions and explorations. Most were small-scale and are not included in today's history books. A few expeditions, however, changed the world forever. Magellan's voyage around the globe was one of them.

The late fifteenth century was a time of great scientific curiosity. It was also a time when European countries were trying to find ways to become richer and more powerful. Royalty invested great sums of money in ventures of exploration for glory, God, and gold. Young boys dreamed of becoming explorers, of getting on board a sailing ship, and heading for the high seas to see what lay beyond the horizon.

Ferdinand Magellan was born to Portuguese nobility in Sabrosa, in northern Portugal. He became a page to Queen Leonor in Lisbon at the age of fourteen. It was as a page that Magellan learned about the famous voyages of Christopher Columbus and Vasco da Gama. These great men inspired Magellan to pursue a life of adventure. He became the first man to sail around the world, and it was he who proved that the earth was round through his expeditions.

The chance to take part in a grand adventure, to be cheered as a hero, and to find great riches—these were the reasons men left the safety of their homes to explore the unknown. Some, like Magellan, also wanted to learn the truth about world geography. Where were other landmasses located? How big were they? Did the oceans all connect? Did different places have different climates? And what about the people and animals who lived in these strange places? There were hundreds of questions to answer, and each answer led to new questions.

Most of the world was unknown to Europeans in 1480, the year Magellan was most likely born. No one knew for certain that Earth was round, although some people in ancient Greece had thought so almost 2,000 years before. Because no one had seen the whole world, people could only guess at its shape. There were all kinds of stories about the mysteries of the world, too: Some people believed that monsters swam in the deep parts of the oceans and that a race of cannibal giants lived on strange islands.

In AD 1000, Vikings from Norway found North America by sailing across the North Atlantic, but they did not explore the continent. Even if they had, other Europeans, such as the Portuguese and the Spanish, wouldn't know much about what the Vikings had found because there was no way for them to communicate. Asians and Polynesians had traveled widely, but they hadn't gone as far west as Europe or to the north.

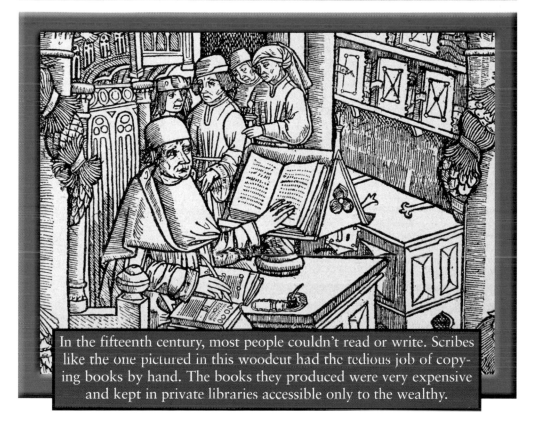

In the fifteenth century, most people couldn't read or write. Scribes like the one pictured in this woodcut had the tedious job of copying books by hand. The books they produced were very expensive and kept in private libraries accessible only to the wealthy.

Why Didn't People Know More About the World?

There were very few books in Europe at that time and practically no libraries. Before the invention of the printing press in 1450, books had to be copied by hand, which took a very long time. Even after books were printed, only a few volumes were printed at a time. Books were kept in universities or monasteries. These libraries were private, open only to the few who were wealthy and educated. Most ordinary people did not know how to read or write anyway.

Very few people traveled even for short distances because it was expensive, uncomfortable, and dangerous. Communication was much, much slower than it is today. Letters took months to get from one country to another. There was no notion of a "global economy," and very few people believed in seeking out anyone outside their own circle of family and friends. They were satisfied to stay at home.

There were no precise maps as we know them today, with distances calculated. For hundreds of years, mapmakers had made fanciful drawings of the world as they imagined it, with sea serpents in the ocean and lands where monsters lived, but they were only guesses, much like today's science fiction stories about life on other planets.

Around 1500, all the new information from the voyages of Christopher Columbus, Bartolomeu Dias, John Cabot, and other explorers was assembled to create a map of the world. The lands new to Europeans included North America, South America, the West Indies, Japan, and China. These maps were interesting to look at, but without any sense of distance, they were not very helpful for navigators.

Other kinds of maps available at that time were charts, which gave information on the depths of oceans around ports. No one had charted the seas more than a couple of miles from shore, however, so the maps didn't help explorers.

This is a detail of a map of the world by the Italian mapmaker Toscanelli.

In 1500, there was no common idea of geography. Germans saw the world in one way, Chinese in another, and Portuguese in yet another. The most important question for them all was whether the oceans were connected. If they were, it would be possible to sail around the world and come into contact with every country with a coastline. No continent, country, or island would be isolated. And someday there would be trade among all nations. Magellan would prove there was a way for these connections to be made.

Problems with Navigation

The first rule of navigation is to know where you are. The second rule is to know where you want to go. Only then can you figure out how to get there. On the open sea, it is impossible to tell where you are if you don't have instruments that measure distance.

Navigation today is a mathematical science, dependent on computerized instruments and sonar, an underwater radar system. But for hundreds of years, it was ·based on experience and eyesight alone. Dead reckoning—guessing where you are based on landmarks—was the most common way to get somewhere. On the open ocean, however, there are no landmarks, but there are signposts in the sky.

In AD 140, an Egyptian named Ptolemy devised a mathematical system for using the stars to determine location. This system is called celestial navigation. Using celestial navigation, sailors could estimate their position by pinpointing the known stars in a clear night sky or, by day, measuring the height of the Sun. This told them how close they were to the equator—the imaginary line that runs around the middle of Earth at 0 degrees latitude. Using this information, they could estimate their ship's latitude if they had a fairly reliable instrument to measure the height of the Sun or a given star. On a cloudy night or stormy day, this method doesn't work.

Ptolemy invented a method to use the stars to determine one's location.

Although the night sky of the Northern Hemisphere was well known to Europeans by Magellan's time, the constellations of the Southern Hemisphere were not. Once his ships got out of familiar territory, they had no celestial signposts to guide them.

This medieval astronomer is using an astronomical device to take measurements from land. As today, ancient sailors relied on navigational tools to find their way across the oceans to explore new lands and return home.

The ancient Greeks thought up the idea of latitude and longitude—dividing Earth up into squares—but it was just a guessing game until proven by navigators. In Magellan's day, longitude could not be determined, in part because no one knew Earth's size. Magellan's contributions to navigation helped make the measurement of longitude possible.

Ptolemy put his system into a book called *Almagest*, which Magellan and most explorers studied and brought with them on their travels. However, Ptolemy underestimated the circumference of Earth. He thought it was 20,000 miles in circumference when it is actually 24,902 miles.

Early navigators were accurate even though they were working with primitive instruments. Sometimes they used an astrolabe ("star taker"). This device was a model of the Ptolemy system that could simulate the position of heavenly bodies in relation to Earth. It was accurate only if it could be kept level and dry.

The astrolabe is an ancient astronomical instrument that shows how the sky looks at a specific place at a given time. A map of the sky was engraved on circular plates that could be rotated, so the navigator could know where a ship was in relation to the stars.

On the deck of a rolling ship, it was usually off by a few degrees. Because they were often made of wood, astrolabes became warped in the humidity of a sea voyage.

13

The most common navigational instrument, and the simplest, was the compass. It came to Europe from China as early as the twelfth century. In its earliest form, it was simply a metal needle that had been rubbed with a lodestone to magnetize it and then set afloat in a cup of water. It always pointed north, toward the North Pole, which is also magnetic. By the fifteenth century, a compass with a movable magnetic needle set on a central pivot was widely used. This is basically the same as the kind of compasses used by hikers and campers today.

Determining the speed of a ship is another important part of navigation. This allows the captain to know how long it will take to reach a certain point and how many supplies to bring. Sailors in Magellan's time figured their ship's speed by tossing a log over the prow (front) of the ship and timing with an hourglass how long it took to reach the stern (back). This very simple system did not produce accurate results, but it gave sailors a general idea of how fast their ship was going.

Kinds of Ships

All the ships during Magellan's time were made of wood. Wood floats, but it also rots. It can break up in a storm and is food for rats and shipworms. Barnacles cling to a wood surface and make it heavier, reducing its speed. All ships were powered by the wind through the use of sails. Smaller boats were powered by manpower: rowing. Steam, gasoline engines, electric batteries, and nuclear power all came much later.

The ships were built for carrying trade goods, not for the comfort of the crew. Around 1470, the major countries of Europe—England, France, Spain, Portugal, Venice (now part of Italy), and Holland—began to build larger merchant ships to search for a trade route to the East. They wanted to reach India, Ceylon, the East Indies, and Malaysia and bring trade goods back to Europe. They could not trade by land, as that would involve costly wars. Instead, they needed to find efficient waterways. This was the reason the great age of discovery began.

This fifteenth-century woodcut depicts Lisbon, Portugal, a major shipping and mercantile center during the Middle Ages and Renaissance. Portuguese explorers sailed from Lisbon on their voyages to Africa and the Americas. Magellan lived here as a young man.

1

EUROPE DISCOVERS THE WORLD

As to the profit of our world from this achievement, East and West alike . . . their people can now exchange their goods.
—Gomes Eanes de Zurara, *The Chronicle of Discovery*, c. 1470

Ferdinand Magellan had three names. He was christened Fernão de Magalhães in his native Portugal. When he moved to Spain, he became Hernando Magallanes. Ferdinand Magellan is the English version of his name. It is not certain when or where Magellan was born because records were not kept then, but we can be reasonably sure he was born in northern Portugal around 1480.

The Portuguese language is very similar to Spanish, but there are enough differences between the two, especially in spelling, to require translation. For instance, San Diego (Spanish) becomes São Diogo in Portuguese. Spain and Portugal had similar customs, religion, and government, but like two high schools in the same town, they were rivals.

Portugal faces the Atlantic Ocean on the Iberian Peninsula in southern Europe. It is a country about half the size of the state of Missouri, and it had a population of about one million people at the time Magellan lived. For most of its history, Portugal has been overshadowed by its much larger neighbor, Spain. When Magellan was alive, Spain and Portugal were bitter enemies.

Across the southern coast of Portugal lies the Strait of Gibraltar and the continent of Africa. The earliest Portuguese navigators turned toward Africa to explore the coastline of that continent. Eventually, Portugal had strongholds all along the coasts of Africa, forcing Spain to seek a westward route.

When Magellan was a boy, his family lived in the small port town of Aveiro, about 150 miles north of Lisbon. Lisbon is the capital city of Portugal and was home of the country's king and queen. Ferdinand's father, Rodrigo, was a sheriff. This was an honorary position—he didn't have to do the work of a sheriff, and the family probably had some money or land inherited from relatives. Like most of Europe, Portugal had a system of nobility that proceeded from the king to dukes and lords and other titles.

The Magellans were considered minor nobility. They had no title, but they were high enough on the social scale for their sons to be educated. The children of common people did not go to school. Magellan's mother was Alda de Mesquita, and nothing is known about her except her name. There were two other children in the family, a girl named Isabel and a boy named Diogo.

Magellan's grandmother on his father's side belonged to the de Sousa family, a noble family favored by the royal house. This was very important to young Ferdinand because it meant he could be appointed to the royal court.

At that time, the royal family controlled everything that went on in the country and all trade with foreign countries. Ambitious young men found it was wise to try to win the favor of the king and queen because that was the only path to wealth and importance in Portugal.

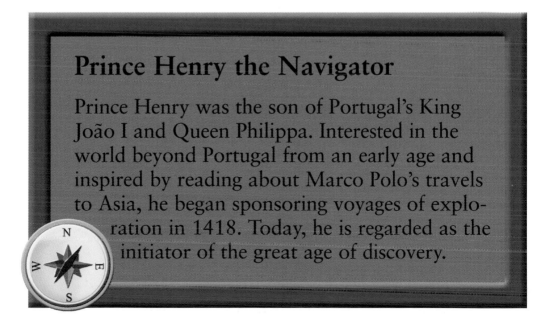

Prince Henry the Navigator

Prince Henry was the son of Portugal's King João I and Queen Philippa. Interested in the world beyond Portugal from an early age and inspired by reading about Marco Polo's travels to Asia, he began sponsoring voyages of exploration in 1418. Today, he is regarded as the initiator of the great age of discovery.

Although little is known about Magellan's boyhood, we can make some educated guesses about it. Because he lived in a small town on an inlet of the ocean and because fishing was an important part of the Portuguese economy, we can imagine that he frequently walked to the docks with friends to watch the fishing boats come in or the trade ships load and unload. Perhaps he talked with sailors and fishermen and heard stories about storms at sea or learned about the kinds of boats tied up at the docks. Perhaps he wondered about what lands lay beyond the horizon or if the ocean went on forever.

The King's Court

When he was about fourteen, Ferdinand, his brother, and a friend named Francisco Serrao went to Lisbon to be pages in the court of King João II and Queen Leonor. João II had become king when Magellan was one year old. He was the great nephew of Prince Henry the Navigator, who had begun the age of discovery. King João II believed, as did his uncle, that Portugal could be a great sea power.

At the court, pages were trained by the queen's brother, Manuel. Manuel saw to it that they were dressed and fed well. Pages were assistants to the royal family. They did errands, learned court manners, and were present at royal

IOANNES II. LVSITANIÆ REX XIII.

King João II of Portugal carried on the overseas expansion policies that his great-uncle, Prince Henry, had begun. He sponsored the exploration of Africa's western coast and the expedition that rounded the tip of Africa, named the Cape of Good Hope. Not satisfied with the revenues he received from trading voyages, João II was determined to establish a Christian empire in West Africa, but he did not achieve this goal.

functions. If they worked hard and made no enemies, they could become apprentices in certain professions. When they graduated, they frequently went into the military as high-ranking officers. They could also receive scholarships and become educated at the university, or they might even become advisers to the king. As long as they stayed on the king's good side, they might be given favors—land and money, or positions as ambassadors to a neighboring royal court.

It was not always easy to stay on the king's good side. There were many courtiers (people who attended the court) and many different kinds of personalities. Some were trusting and kind, others were hostile or jealous. As Magellan found out, it was impossible to please everyone at court. Loyalties shifted from day to day. Someone who was a friend on Monday could be an enemy by Thursday. Some people who thought they'd been slighted never forgave or forgot the offense; others didn't let anything bother them. His good spirit allowed Magellan to advance to higher positions.

Manuel and King João II did not trust each other and frequently were at odds. Magellan was loyal to the king and obeyed him, even when that made Manuel angry. In 1495, João II died, and because the king had no son, Manuel became the king. As king, Manuel remembered that Magellan had preferred João II, and Manuel carried this grudge for the rest of his life.

While he was a student, Magellan learned reading, writing, religion, arithmetic, music, dancing, horsemanship, and fencing—the gentleman's way of solving arguments. He also studied algebra, geometry, astronomy, and navigation, all of which helped him to develop the skills he would need on his expeditions.

After Magellan finished his time as a page, he became a paid palace employee. He probably worked as a clerk for the India House, the agency that regulated trade. In the India House building, next door to the palace, maps, ships' logs, and reports of voyages were stored. As a clerk, Magellan would have been able to study them. He also would have learned how to outfit an expedition. By reading the accounts of other voyages, he could decide which instruments, arms, supplies, and goods for trade would be needed.

He may have come across information about a strait between two oceans. The strait was something he had wanted to find for a long time; he thought it would be shorter, easier, and calmer than taking the route around the tip of South America. It was not known at the time if a route around South America was even possible. It might have been that South America went all the way to the South Pole, as many people thought at the time.

Because of the encouragement of King João II and then of King Manuel, Lisbon was a center for trade. Ships of many nationalities crowded the docks with flags from Holland, England, Belgium, France, Greece, and Germany. African slaves were also evident. In fact, Portugal is credited with starting the slave trade.

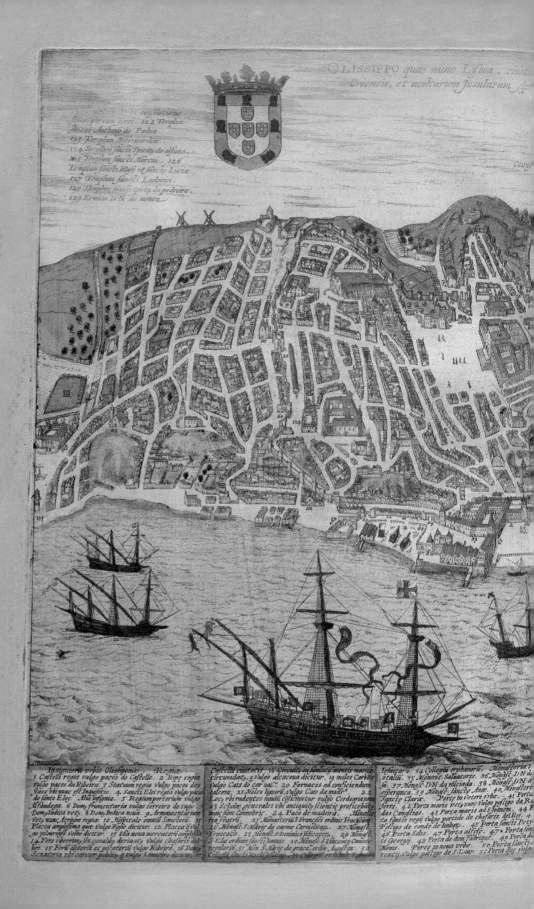

Lisbon was founded by Phoenicians, who established a trading post there. It soon became a convenient port of call for ships sailing from the Mediterranean Sea to northern Europe. Because of its large, deep harbor, Lisbon attracted hefty trading ships and led the way in trading and exploration during the Renaissance. It became the capital of Portugal in 1256.

Everyone in Lisbon, including Magellan, would have heard of the successful voyage of Christopher Columbus in 1492, the journey of John Cabot to the New World in 1497, and Portugal's own Vasco da Gama and his voyages to India. Magellan was probably in the excited crowd on the docks in 1499 when two of da Gama's ships returned to Lisbon from India. One ship was loaded with spices, rare woods, and jewels, all purchased in Indian markets.

In 1500, when Magellan was twenty years old, the Portuguese explorer Pedro Álvares Cabral and his fleet of thirteen ships reached the coast of South America. Cabral claimed the land for Portugal, naming it Brazil for the brazilwood they found there. Magellan would have heard stories of the strange creatures in Brazil and seen the maps that Cabral made of his journey.

All of these stories of exploration, in addition to the emphasis on trade in Lisbon, influenced Magellan's decision to lead a life on the sea.

2

THE SPICE WARS

*Here ships can get shelter against every wind . . .
and in the same way they can go out with every wind,
whenever the seamen willeth it.*
—Gomes Eanes de Zurara, *The Chronicle of Discovery*, c. 1470

At the time Magellan moved to Lisbon, kingdoms wanted spices just as nations want oil today. Spices were used for more than flavoring food, although that was one use. In the days before indoor plumbing and concern for personal hygiene, people perfumed the air with spices.

Owning spices was a status symbol for the wealthy. Nutmeg, for instance, was as sought after as the finest perfumes are today. Wealthy people would bring their own silver nutmeg graters with them when they went out to dinner, wearing them like jewelry to show them off.

The traffic in spices goes back to before recorded history. During the age of exploration, European merchants realized that spice-producing regions could be reached by ship. First Portugal, then Spain, England, Holland, and eventually even the newly founded United States entered one of history's most exciting contests. For four centuries, the major Western powers raced each other to the Orient and battled for control of the spice-producing lands. Portugal claimed Ceylon, the East Indies, and the Spice Islands, and for a time the spice trade made it one of the richest nations in Europe.

Many spices were used as medicine. Twenty-six different spices appeared in prescriptions for various diseases. Cloves were a remedy for chest coughs, headaches, and earaches. (Today oil of cloves is frequently used for toothaches.) Some spices were also thought to be a protection against contagious diseases. By sprinkling powdered cloves on their clothes, people thought they could keep away colds and the flu.

Spices had another practical use. In the days before refrigeration, food spoiled easily because there was no way to keep it cold. Some spices were used in food preservation; they made dried food taste better and last longer before it spoiled.

Wanting spices was just part of the desire for the good life. Wealthy people also wanted jewelry, silks, tapestries, fine porcelain (china), and anything else that seemed luxurious and made them feel important. These things were not available in Portugal or anywhere in Europe. They had to come from the East. Merchants could see that there was a fortune to be made in trade.

Arabian traders had a monopoly on the spice trade in the fifteenth century. The main market for Eastern goods was Alexandria, Egypt. In order to keep their supplies a secret, Eastern traders wouldn't tell Europeans where their spices came from. Instead, they made up fantastic stories about their locations, saying they grew in dangerous places and were guarded by terrible beasts.

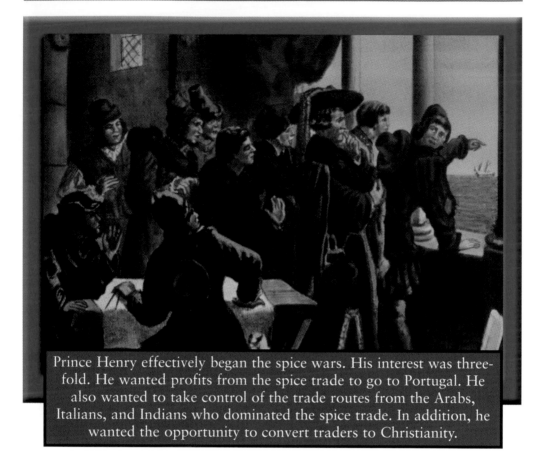

Prince Henry effectively began the spice wars. His interest was three-fold. He wanted profits from the spice trade to go to Portugal. He also wanted to take control of the trade routes from the Arabs, Italians, and Indians who dominated the spice trade. In addition, he wanted the opportunity to convert traders to Christianity.

But European traders didn't believe these stories. They heard rumors of islands somewhere in the Indian Ocean, where spices—especially nutmeg, mace, and cloves—grew abundantly on trees and bushes. All one had to do was go there, pluck off the seeds, and fill up the holds of ships. Then they could sail back to Europe and become very wealthy.

The Spice Islands came to be called the Moluccas. Today they are part of Indonesia. The Indian Ocean lies between the coast of eastern Africa and Malaysia, Indonesia, and Australia, which form a barrier to the east. All of the lands in the Indian Ocean—the hundreds of islands as well as the sub-continent of India and southwest Asia—were then called the East Indies.

Prince Henry set the course for Portuguese spice hunters. He felt that all the spices of the Orient should come to Lisbon, bringing prosperity to Portugal. The Portuguese wanted to control the East Indies not only for the trade goods but also to convert the natives to Christianity. Their strategy was to defeat the alliance of Arabs, Italians, and Indians that already controlled the spice trade in India. Their first step was to use force to set up military bases at points around India and the east coast of Africa.

In 1505, at the age of twenty-five, Magellan joined the "spice wars." King Manuel named Dom Francisco de Almeida the first Portuguese viceroy (governor) of the Indies. Magellan sailed as a general hand with Almeida's fleet, which contained twenty-two ships and 1,500 men. Their goal was to explore and conquer India.

In their attempt at conquest, the Portuguese fought several battles with the Arabs and Indians. Magellan was wounded twice in battle, in 1506 and in 1509. He earned a reputation as a brave fighter. He was promoted to captain in 1510 and took part in expeditions that captured the kingdom of Malacca in the Malay Peninsula in 1511.

The Gateway to the Far East

With their capture of Malacca in 1511, the Portuguese won control of the gateway to the Far East, shattering the centuries-old Arabian monopoly. By then, the Portuguese were in control of the spice trade of the Malabar Coast of India, Ceylon, Java, and Sumatra, where they fought with the Arabs for control of the pepper trade. From India and Ceylon, they brought cardamom, cinnamon, and ginger.

Magellan spent about a year in Malacca, gathering information from merchants and from the crews of junks (Chinese ships) anchored in the harbor. Here he learned that his boyhood friend, Francisco Serrao, had found the Spice Islands and was living there. He had even married a daughter of the sultan (king). Serrao sent Magellan a letter telling him how wonderful the islands were and how great the opportunities were for trading.

In Malacca, Magellan acquired a slave named Enrique, who stayed with him for the rest of his life. Apparently, Enrique knew many languages because he served as translator for Magellan. He may have been born in the Philippine Islands, as he gave Magellan much valuable information about that area.

MOLVQVES

PETITE
IAVE

GRANDE IAVE

Consisting of a group of about 1,000 islands, the Moluccas were known as the "Spice Islands" during Magellan's time. Valuable cloves, nutmeg, and mace were in great supply on the Spice Islands, and they were of great interest to the many European nations that tried to gain control of the area. Although the Spanish, Portuguese, English, and Dutch all raced to claim the islands, it was the Dutch who eventually won out. By the end of the eighteenth century, however, the Moluccas were no longer economically prosperous. After World War II they were incorporated into the state of East Indonesia, which was made part of the Republic of Indonesia in 1949.

Before Magellan could join his friend in the Moluccas, King Manuel sent Magellan to Morocco in North Africa, along with 15,000 Portuguese soldiers, to put down a rebellion by the Moors. Magellan was badly wounded in a battle in the small town of Azamor; a lance pierced his knee. He limped because of this injury for the rest of his life. European soldiers wore armor then, but usually they did not wear leg armor in battle because it was so heavy and bulky that it slowed them down.

To Clear Up Confusion

Three separate places with similar sounding names were important to Magellan when he was young:

- Malacca is in Malaysia, along the sea route between India and China. Magellan was part of the army that captured the city in 1511.

- Morocco is a country in North Africa. Magellan was badly wounded there in a battle against the Moors.

- The Moluccas are the Spice Islands and are now part of Indonesia. Magellan wanted to find them and open up the spice trade for Portugal.

For his bravery in this fight, Magellan was promoted to quartermaster-major. This was a prestigious post, and some of the older officers were jealous. That may have been the reason why officials charged Magellan with illegally trading with the Muslim Moors a few years later. This was a very serious charge because it amounted to treason—the Moors were enemies of the Portuguese. Magellan claimed he was innocent. After an investigation, the army agreed, and the charges against him were dropped.

The idea that Magellan, with his strong Catholic background, would trade with Muslims was almost impossible to comprehend. The hostility between Christians and Muslims was intense at the time. Each group believed that theirs was the one true religion. Each accused the other of being infidels (nonbelievers), even devils. Christians didn't consider it a sin to kill Muslims any more than Muslims considered it sinful to kill Christians. On the contrary, such murders were considered pleasing to God or Allah. Furthermore, the Moors had invaded Portugal in the eighth century and had remained there for 400 years. The Portuguese battled long and hard to get them out. Even by 1500, they had not forgotten their struggle.

Although the idea that Magellan was a traitor was unlikely, King Manuel still held a grudge against him. He acted as if he believed the charges and fired Magellan from government service. Terribly disappointed, bewildered, and resentful, Magellan realized the king would never allow him to head an expedition to the Spice Islands. His career as a Portuguese explorer was over.

Unwilling to swallow his pride and move back to the town where he grew up, Magellan gave up his Portuguese citizenship, moved to Spain, and began a new life there. Although he was without family and friends and the comforts of home, he was about to make history.

3

THE EXPEDITION
TAKES SHAPE

When . . . the Spanish in the west and the Portuguese in the east began to search for new and unknown lands, their own kings . . . divided the whole globe between them by the authority . . . of Pope Alexander the Sixth.
—Letter from Maximilian of Transylvania, 1523

When Magellan moved to Spain in 1517, Spain and Portugal were in a bitter "race for discovery." Years earlier, Pope Alexander VI had tried to stop the competition by drawing a "line of demarcation," later known as the Treaty of Tordesillas in 1494. This imaginary line divided the known world in half, giving all lands discovered east of the line to Portugal and all lands west to Spain. (Other European countries, such as England and France, were not yet in the running.)

Although Europeans knew where the Spice Islands (Moluccas) were by 1517, no officially sponsored expedition had landed there to claim them. The Treaty of Tordesillas stated that if the islands were discovered by going east, they belonged to Portugal. If they were discovered and held from the west, they belonged to Spain.

Holy Roman Emperor Charles V was the king of Spain, Germany, the Netherlands, Austria, and the Spanish-American colonies from 1519 to 1558. His goal was to become leader of a global empire, and during his rule, he greatly expanded the Spanish empire in the New World. But the human and financial costs of his constant warfare drained Spanish resources, and his hopes for a global empire under Spain were crushed by the rise of other powers in western Europe.

From the time of Christopher Columbus's voyages beginning in 1492, Spain had a good reputation for supporting explorers. King Ferdinand and Queen Isabella had organized the Casa de Contratacíon ("House of Trade") to license all ships, whether for trade or exploration. The Casa also decided where ships would go and who would be aboard them. The Casa was made up of Spanish merchants who were very interested in getting to the Spice Islands before the Portuguese.

Magellan knew he had to make friends with the men in the Casa. He stayed with Diego Barbosa, an important official in Seville who may have been an old friend. Barbosa was one of Magellan's strongest supporters and introduced him to many Casa members.

Soon after moving to Spain, Magellan married Beatriz Barbosa, Diego's daughter, proving that he intended to stay. Although they were not married long before he left for his voyage, he generously provided for her and their infant son, Rodrigo, in his will. (He also left 10 percent of all his assets— a tithe—to the Catholic Church.)

In February 1518, Magellan felt he was ready to approach the king with his proposal to find the Spice Islands. He and Ruy Faleiro, a Portuguese cosmographer (star mapper), journeyed to the Spanish court at Valladolid in the region of Castile to seek the help of King Charles I.

Charles was only sixteen years old when his grandfather, King Ferdinand, died. As heir to the throne, Charles was brought to Spain from Belgium, where he had been attending school. When Magellan approached him, he was eighteen and had been in Spain less than six months. His intelligence made up for his lack of experience, and he was very interested in learning more about exploration. (In 1519, he would become Charles V, Holy Roman Emperor over most of Europe.)

On the way to Valladolid, the impulsive Faleiro argued with the levelheaded Magellan about how they would petition the king. Faleiro seemed to be more interested in enriching himself than in bringing glory to Spain. The men were joined by a man named Armanda, who was a merchant from the Casa. Armanda thought Faleiro, who suffered periods of madness, acted foolishly, and he distrusted him.

Most of the Spanish merchants supported Magellan's plan. Not only would it enrich Spain, but it would also keep Portugal from getting richer. Although these merchants had supported Columbus during his first two voyages, he had disappointed them. He had brought them no new rich markets. They thought Magellan's voyage would be more successful. In addition, many merchants favored Magellan's down-to-earth personality.

In Portugal, meanwhile, King Manuel had changed his mind about Magellan. He was finally willing to listen to Magellan's proposal. But it was too late: Magellan refused to return, even though he heard that Portuguese agents would try to stop him from sailing under a Spanish flag.

Magellan's presentation on February 23, 1518, impressed everyone at the court of King Charles I. The would-be explorer brought maps, charts, letters of support

On September 27, 1513, while on an expedition to Panama, Balboa climbed alone to the peak of a mountain and for the first time saw the "South Sea," or what is now known as the Pacific Ocean, and claimed it for Portugal.

from geographers, and specific plans. He demonstrated Faleiro's new methods of celestial navigation. He didn't make wild promises, as other explorers had done. He stood straight like a trained soldier and looked everyone in the eye.

He said he wanted to find "Balboa's Sea" (the Pacific Ocean), which he thought would take him to the Spice Islands. A few years earlier, the explorer Vasco Nuñez de Balboa had glimpsed the ocean

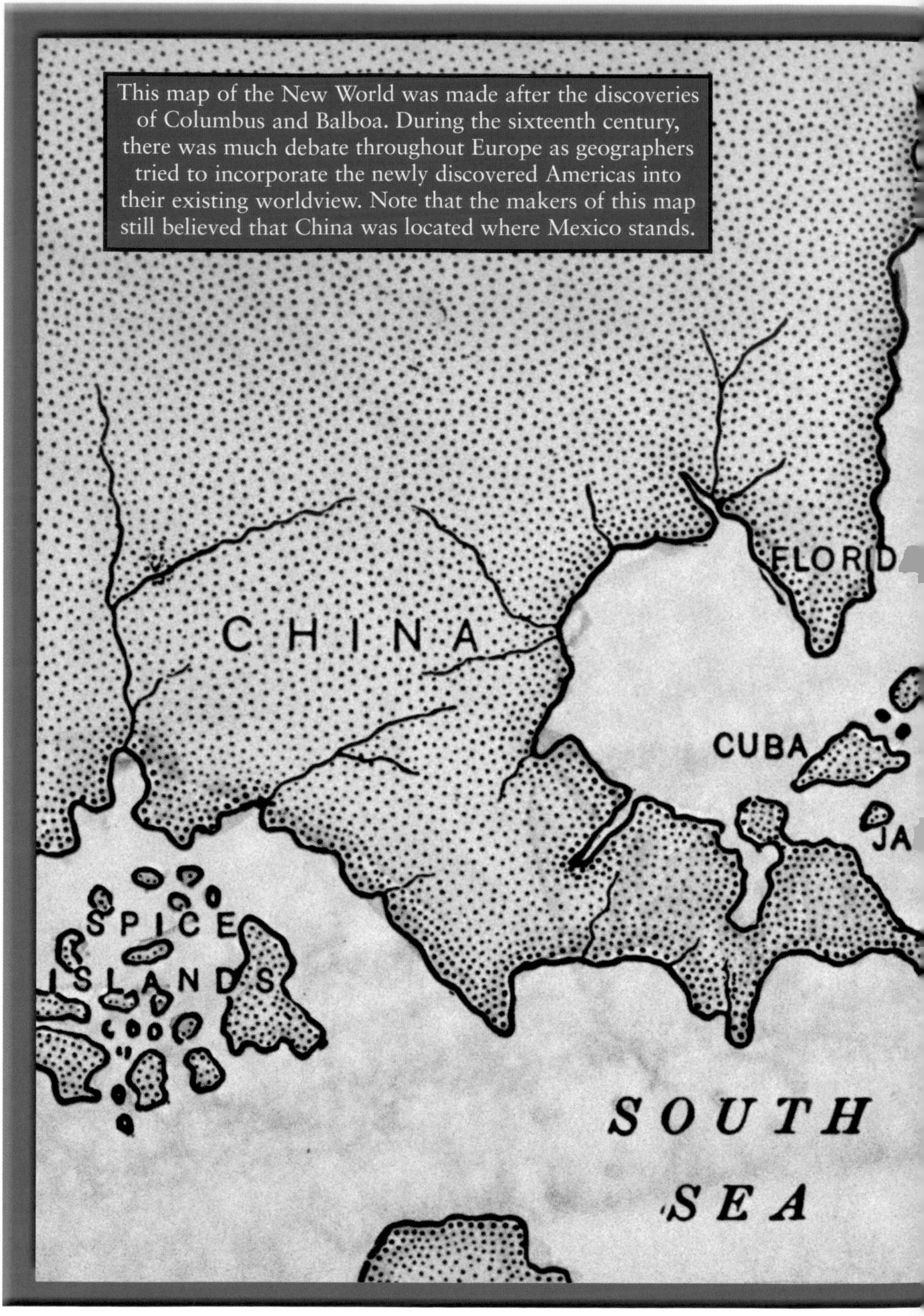

This map of the New World was made after the discoveries of Columbus and Balboa. During the sixteenth century, there was much debate throughout Europe as geographers tried to incorporate the newly discovered Americas into their existing worldview. Note that the makers of this map still believed that China was located where Mexico stands.

CHINA

FLORID

CUBA

JA

SPICE
ISLANDS

SOUTH

SEA

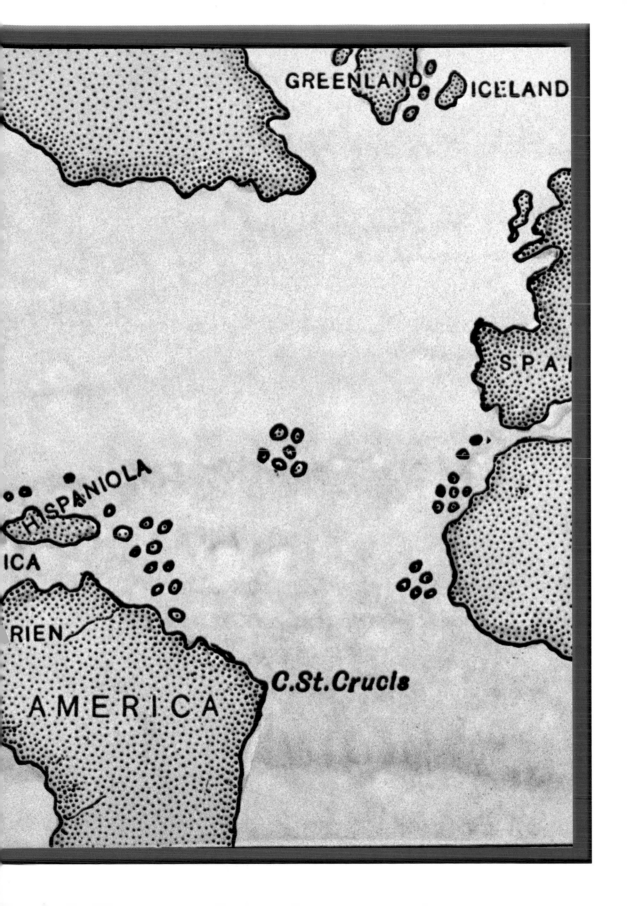

from a mountaintop in what is now Panama. He could tell it was a different body of water than the one he had sailed across (the Atlantic) to get to South America. A report from another exploration off the coast of Brazil had convinced Magellan that any southwest passage to Balboa's Sea would be west of the line of demarcation. If such a passage existed, it would belong to Spain, not Portugal.

Magellan presented his ideas with authority. Columbus had spent seven years trying to win the support of the Spanish crown; it took Magellan only one month. On March 22, 1518, King Charles agreed to Magellan's proposal.

Magellan and Faleiro were appointed joint captains general of an expedition directed to seek a Spanish route to the Moluccas. They were given the authority to govern any lands they discovered and were to receive a one-twentieth share of the net profits from their venture. (Eventually, Faleiro was judged too high-strung to be allowed on a ship and was dropped from the roster.)

Preparations for the Expedition

The Spanish merchant Armanda bought five well-worn merchant ships (carracks) for the expedition. They were named *Victoria*, *Concepción*, *San Antonio*, *Santiago*, and *Trinidad*, the flagship. The ships were small but wide in the beam, built to hold trading goods.

This is a hand-colored woodcut of Magellan's carrack the *Victoria*. Compared with other carracks, the *Victoria* was quite small. The generally spacious vessels offered room for a large crew and provisions, as well as for cargo to be brought back home.

Each ship had three masts: main, foremast, and mizzenmast. A bowsprit was carried in case an additional sail was needed. Most of the sails used were square, but there were also a few lateen, or triangular, ones. The ships carried longboats and launches, which were stowed on the main deck and took up a lot of room. These rowboats were used as taxis to go from one ship to another or to go from the ship to the shore.

The decks and holds were stocked with gear, supplies, gifts for the people they would meet, and armaments. Among their arms were cannons, 5,600 pounds of gunpowder, arquebuses (old-fashioned rifles), swords, javelins, lances, cross-bows, and more than 4,200 arrows.

Their food was very plain—salted meat, rice, biscuits, beans, almonds, and raisins. They brought salted fish and cheese for special occasions. Barrels of water and wine were stored above and below decks.

The navigation instruments didn't take up much room. Among the five ships, there were twenty-three parchment charts, six pairs of compasses (and thirty-five extra needles), twenty-one wooden quadrants, seven astrolabes, and eighteen hourglasses.

For the natives they expected to meet, they brought mirrors, knives, fishhooks, velvet, ivory, brass bracelets, and, the most popular item, small bells. They carried 20,000 bells.

Magellan supervised the hiring of the crew. Some were his choice (thirty Portuguese seamen, for instance); others were appointed by the Casa. The five ships had a combined total of about 270 men of

Travelers from all over the world converged on the port of Lisbon during the sixteenth century. Lisbon has been the main gateway to Portugal for well over 1,000 years and continues to be one of Europe's leading seaports. The port of Lisbon is a natural deep-water harbor located on the Tagus River near the Atlantic coast.

various ethnic groups, mostly Spanish. There were also men from England, Asia, Ireland, Greece, Portugal, France, and Italy. The smallest crew, made up of thirty-two men, was on the *Santiago*; the largest crew, sixty men, was on the *Trinidad*.

Most of the crew were ordinary seamen, but there were also barbers (who acted as doctors in addition to cutting hair), chaplains, coopers (who repaired barrels and did carpentry), caulkers, and gunners. These men signed on because they needed work.

The officers, on the other hand, had different motives for joining the expedition. Most wanted to become wealthy and powerful and to work their way up to become court favorites. Two officers are remembered today for their part in the voyage: Juan Sebastian de Elcano (or del Cano), who was originally the master of the *Concepción*, and Juan de Cartagena, who had the command of the *San Antonio*. Cartagena hoped to become inspector general of the whole fleet, with Magellan under him. Instead, King Charles made Magellan knight commander, a post of honor, with the title captain general. Cartagena never got over his disappointment. He refused to acknowledge Magellan's authority and tried to get the other Spanish officers to disobey him as well.

Also on board was Antonio Pigafetta, an Italian, who may have been a spy for his government or simply a sightseer. Pigafetta kept an extensive diary that tells us much about the voyage and Magellan, although some things he wrote about are too fantastic to be believed today. In his diary, he wrote that he wanted to go with the expedition because he was "desirous of seeing the wonderful things of the ocean."

It took many months to get the ships outfitted in Seville. On August 10, 1519, the five ships left Seville and sailed down the Guadalquivir River to the port of San Lúcar. They stayed in this port for more than a month, making further preparations. Finally, Magellan was satisfied and gave his crew the order to get under way. Balboa's Sea awaited them.

4

THE VOYAGE BEGINS

Their course would be this, to sail westward, coasting the southern hemisphere to the East. The thing seemed almost impossible and useless.
—Letter from Maximilian of Transylvania, 1523

Before dawn on September 21, 1519, Magellan's voyage began. With sails billowing, the ships left the port of San Lúcar on a southwestern course toward Africa.

After six days at sea, the convoy stopped at the Canary Islands, about seventy miles from northwestern Africa, just as Columbus had done. There the ships took on meat, water, wood, and pitch (tar) for making the wooden ships watertight. The seven islands and six islets that make up the Canaries had been under Spanish rule since 1479 and served as a way station for Spanish navigators.

Magellan left Spain in 1519 with five ships and about 270 men. He hoped to reach the Spice Islands by sailing west. After many failed attempts, they finally found the strait that is now named after Magellan. They struggled through the treacherous passage for thirty-eight days before finally reaching the Pacific Ocean.

While they were still in the Canaries, a ship arrived from San Lúcar with an urgent message for Magellan from his father-in-law, Diego Barbosa. Barbosa warned Magellan that some of his captains had bragged while they were still in Seville that they would remove Magellan from his command one way or another.

Magellan sent a reply back. He wrote that he would give his captains no cause to revolt against him. Instead, he would listen to their complaints and try to resolve whatever was bothering them. He wanted to cooperate with everyone on the voyage. Barbosa showed this reply to members of the Casa, and they liked Magellan's coolheadedness. Showing it to them was a wise decision. When problems later arose between Magellan and his officers, the court knew that Magellan had tried to be fair.

As soon as the five ships were well stocked, they left the Canary Islands. Because of the warning from his father-in-law, Magellan decided not to tell the officers in the other ships of his exact route. He told them simply to follow him—to follow his flag by day and the lanterns on the ship by night. When the ocean was calm, the men on board the different ships often shouted information to each other. There was no other system of communication, not even the use of signal flags. Not being told where they were going angered the captains, but they followed Magellan's lead for the first several weeks.

Life at Sea

Once they were under sail, the sailors kept to a strict shipboard routine. Discipline was a crucial part of life at sea. Every crew member was given a job and was expected to do it well and without complaint. Idlers were punished.

As captain general, Magellan had authority over everyone, including the other captains. Each ship captain had authority on his ship over the duties assigned there. The master oversaw the housekeeping details on the ship, keeping it clean and in good repair, and the mate assigned chores to the seamen to keep the ship seaworthy.

The ships were steered by a tiller that extended from the rudder through an opening in the stern. The man who controlled the tiller was called the helmsman. He worked below the deck and could not see out, so the pilot on the quarterdeck shouted commands to him through a hatch. In setting the course, the pilot used dead reckoning (watching where he was going and using landmarks) and also received instructions from the captain based on star charts.

The crew was divided up into watches. They had to watch for anything and everything, since they had no radar. Did that cloud on the horizon look like an approaching storm? Was that disturbance in the water a whale that might collide with the ship? Were other ships nearby? Once they started moving into uncharted waters, they had to be especially attentive, for no one knew what to expect.

One four-hour watch was assigned to the port (left) side of the ship and another to starboard (right). The crew used sand clocks, or hourglasses, to time their watches. Each sand clock took thirty minutes to empty, so for a four-hour watch, it had to be turned eight times. It was against regulations for a sailor to hold the hourglass because the warmth of his body made the sand run faster and the time of his watch shorter.

The captain always took the first watch of the night. At the end of his watch, a mate sang a song:

On deck, on deck, gentlemen of the starboard watch,
Hurry up on deck, Mr. Pilot's watch,
Right now; get up, get up, get up!

The daytime work for the sailors was never-ending, especially swabbing (mopping) the deck to keep it free of salt water and pumping out the bilges. The bilges were the areas below the waterline where dirty water collected. Too much water could sink the ship. Sailors also had to take care of the sails and the rigging—the system of ropes that kept the sails in place. A torn sail or frayed rope had to be repaired at once. Sailors were constantly searching for leaks, damage done by rats and shipworms, and any other signs of trouble. Their lives depended on keeping the vessels "shipshape."

Life at sea was difficult and often deadly for sailors. Each man was kept busy making sure the ship was in order. The sailors often did not get enough sleep or food.

There were no cooks on board. When the weather was good enough, apprentice seamen cooked on deck over a sand bed in the firebox. When the weather was bad, meals were catch-as-catch-can for the seamen. Cabin boys, who were like domestic servants, prepared meals for the officers.

The only person with any privacy was the captain, who had a small cabin in the forecastle in front. The men slept on deck where and when they could. When the weather was bad, they sometimes went for days without sleeping at all.

Under Magellan's command, formal religious services were conducted by either a chaplain or the captain every day on each of the ships. This was not true for other expeditions.

The Voyage Continues

As they headed south toward the equator, the five ships kept close to the coast of Africa to avoid the Portuguese-held Cape Verde Islands. Magellan feared an attack by his former countrymen to stop the voyage.

They passed the landmark mountain of Sierra Leone on the western coast of Africa, and then it began to rain in furious squalls. It rained so hard and for so many days that the expedition's stores began to mold and rot. Magellan put the crew on half-rations to conserve the food.

During one particularly bad storm, the men saw Saint Elmo's fire—a phenomenon of atmospheric electricity that sometimes gathers about the masthead of ships and on riggings. Although similar to lightning, Saint Elmo's fire forms cloudlike shapes rather than zigzags in the sky. In Magellan's day, these shapes were interpreted as religious signs—a cross or the face of a saint, for instance. The men took the appearance of Saint

Elmo's fire as a good omen, and, indeed, after the sighting the sea became calm. Unfortunately, it was too calm, and the ships became stuck in the doldrums, where the wind did not blow. For weeks they progressed only a few miles a day riding the ocean waves.

By sailing in a diagonal line across the Atlantic, they reached the coast of Brazil in November. This area was familiar to Magellan from the stories he'd heard of earlier explorations. He'd studied the maps of the coast while he had been in Lisbon.

They sailed into the beautiful natural harbor of Rio de Janeiro. There they saw parrots, monkeys, and other exotic animals and plants they had heard about. The friendly natives—the Tamojos—had known the earlier Portuguese explorers and swarmed onto the decks of the ships offering chickens, fish, and garden produce in exchange for fishhooks, knives, combs, or mirrors. One small bell was traded for a whole basket of sweet potatoes.

Although the men enjoyed warm, sunny Brazil, Magellan was nervous about being in Portuguese territory. He was always on the lookout for Portuguese ships. He hurried the men through their repair work, and on Christmas Eve, the

When Magellan and his crew sailed into the harbor of Rio de Janeiro, they were stunned by its natural beauty. They encountered animals and plants they had never seen before. The native people, the Tamojos, were friendly and willing to trade.

ships were again ready for sea. The Feast of the Nativity was celebrated on board. The next morning, the fleet headed west by southwest under full sail. Then the exploration part of the voyage began. The eastern coast of South America was new to Magellan and everyone else. He was determined to explore every inlet carefully in search of the passage to Balboa's Sea.

5

THE EXPLORATION

Geographers . . . crowd into the edges of their maps parts of the world which they do not know about.
—Plutarch, *Lives*, c. AD 100

The line of demarcation gave the eastern part of Brazil to Portugal. Once Magellan passed that point, he was safe from Portuguese attack and free to claim all he saw for Spain and King Charles.

The ships proceeded very slowly down the eastern coast of South America, and the pilots made careful notations in their logbooks of exactly where they were according to the star charts. Magellan still did not trust his officers well enough to tell them his plans, and three of the captains became increasingly angry with him because he was so secretive. They feared he planned to meet Portuguese agents somewhere, betray Spain, and give over command of the voyage to them, although the opposite was true.

In the Southern Hemisphere, Magellan encountered high seas and ocean storms that caused damage to his ship. To avoid dangerous winter weather, he landed on what he named Patagonia.

When they came to the Rio del Plata, between today's Argentina and Uruguay, Magellan hoped it was the passage through South America because it was so wide. He sent the *Santiago* to investigate. Two weeks later, the ship came back with the disappointing news that the Rio del Plata was simply a river.

It was now mid-March, the beginning of winter in the Southern Hemisphere. They were below 45 degrees latitude, sailing toward the South Pole. (The equivalent spot in the Northern Hemisphere would be Chicago.) The men were not prepared for winter. Most of them came from the Mediterranean area, where it was always warm. Storm followed storm, and the ships were showing damage. Magellan knew they had to find a place to stay for the winter, protected from the storms and near a source of food.

Magellan found a place and named this area of the Argentine coast Patagonia—Spanish for "big feet"—because of the large natives that they saw. Antonio Pigafetta recalled that an earlier explorer of Brazil wrote of these natives, "They swear that the footprints left upon the sand show them to have feet twice as large as those of a medium-sized man." Later explorers estimated that these native people were between six and seven feet tall. If so, they would have appeared as giants to the men of southern Europe, who were much shorter than most men are today, probably under five feet five inches tall.

Mutiny

Meanwhile, Magellan's relationship with Captain Cartagena had gotten worse. One day, Cartagena was especially rude to Magellan in front of the other officers. Magellan ordered him arrested and took away his command of the *San Antonio*. He imprisoned Cartagena on the deck of the *Trinidad*, where he could watch him. The captain of the *Victoria* begged Magellan to put Cartagena in his custody, and Magellan consented, saying that the captain must promise that Cartagena would be kept on the ship. The captain agreed but then let Cartagena go ashore once they reached Brazil. Magellan arrested him again and transferred him to the *Concepcíon*.

As they sailed south, Cartagena complained about the cold, lack of food, storms, and uncertainty of where they were headed. He pressed the other officers to insist to Magellan that they return to Spain. Magellan said he would not even consider returning home. He felt that would be a slap in the face to King Charles and the Casa, who had invested so much in this voyage. He could not disappoint them. He told the officers he would rather die because he prized honor above all else, including comfort.

On March 31, the convoy turned into a bay at 49 degrees south. (Winnipeg, Manitoba, is at 49 degrees north.) Magellan knew they couldn't stand the cold if they went farther south, so he decided they would stay in this harbor, which he named Port San Julián.

Furious at the decision, Cartagena attempted a mutiny, telling the men that Magellan was leading them to destruction. He promised them that they would get food and could go back to Spain if they followed him. Even though they wanted to go home, most of the men were loyal to Magellan. He was able to end the mutiny after only a few hours.

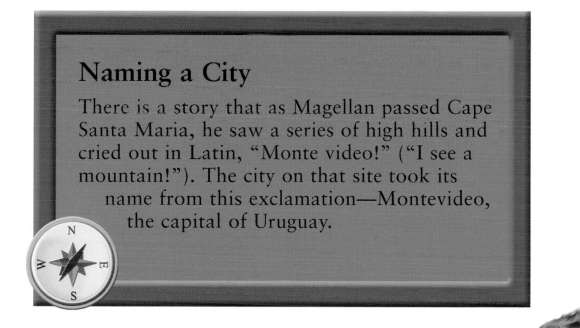

Naming a City

There is a story that as Magellan passed Cape Santa Maria, he saw a series of high hills and cried out in Latin, "Monte video!" ("I see a mountain!"). The city on that site took its name from this exclamation—Montevideo, the capital of Uruguay.

Magellan immediately called a court martial for Cartagena and the men who supported him. Magellan did not preside over the trial; instead, a Spanish captain did. This was a wise move on Magellan's part. Cartagena and the mutineers were found guilty by a fellow countryman. One captain was sentenced to death. Cartagena was imprisoned. Almost forty other seamen were chained and sentenced to hard labor.

There was much labor to be done at Port San Julián. They had to clean and repair the ships and consolidate the supplies. Rotten boards were replaced, seams were caulked, and the hulls were tarred. An inventory of the supplies showed that the sailors had been cheated in Seville and had only half of what they should have. Their food supply would last only another six months.

It's difficult to understand why the men were unable to get food on shore. There were ostriches, llamas, rabbits, and other animals around, but the men had no success in hunting. Perhaps they were afraid to risk tasting the fruit, nuts, or roots they found, or perhaps they didn't find any. There was little freshwater to replenish their barrels; instead, the water they found was salty and undrinkable.

Juan de Cartagena, commander of the *San Antonio*, wanted to be the inspector general of Magellan's entire fleet, but King Charles made Magellan knight commander. Cartagena never got over his resentment, which led him to attempt a mutiny while the fleet was at Port San Julián. He was court martialed, found guilty, and put into stocks.

When Magellan realized they had enough food for only a few more months, he knew they couldn't spend the whole winter in Port San Julián. They had to find a way to get to the western ocean and the Spice Islands, even though the weather was against them. It was so cold that many men suffered from frostbitten hands, and several men froze to death.

Cartagena tried one more time to get the men to mutiny. This time they were disgusted with him and didn't listen. Magellan sentenced him to be marooned. He and one other sailor were deposited on the coast of Patagonia with their swords and some food. Cartagena was never heard from again.

Before they left Port San Julián, Magellan sent the *Santiago* to explore a river inlet to the south. The ship ran into a violent squall that ripped off its sails. The crew was able to jump off onto the nearby beach. Minutes later, the ship was pounded to pieces in the surf. There were only four ships remaining. For eight days, the shipwrecked sailors collected timber from the ship, planning to make a raft large enough to carry all of them back to Port San Julián. Weak with cold and hunger, they couldn't do it. Instead, they built a two-man raft, and the two strongest men were chosen for the journey. It took them eleven days to reach Magellan, and when they reached camp, they were so thin no one recognized them. Magellan sent a rescue party to bring back the other crewmen.

On August 24, the fleet left Port San Julián and continued south to an inlet they named Santa Cruz. Here they found fish and seals to hunt. They enjoyed watching the penguins, which they called ducks. For the moment they had enough food. They spent the winter in the bay, then left on October 18.

On October 21, the lookout spotted an opening that looked like a bay. The ships sailed in to investigate. The *San Antonio* and the *Concepcíon* went ahead to explore while the *Trinidad* and *Victoria* waited. When they were satisfied that this was the passage to the sea, the first two ships returned with pennants flying, crews cheering, and guns firing.

Magellan named the passage All Saints Channel, but it would be forever known as the Strait of Magellan. Although Magellan and his crew had great hopes that it would be an easy passage to Balboa's Sea, it was not. It took them thirty-eight days to maneuver through the 334-mile strait, bucking high winds and bitter cold. They were surrounded by rock cliffs and snow-capped mountains. It looked like a place where no one could survive. But on the land to the south of them, they could see campfires burning at night. They named this area Tierra del Fuego, or "land of fire." This is the southernmost tip of South America.

This artist's depiction of Magellan's fleet sailing into Tierra del Fuego is full of religious and mystical imagery. Tierra del Fuego was named for the fires (fuego) lit along the shore by the native people who lived there. It consists of one large island (sometimes called simply Tierra del Fuego), five medium-sized islands, and numerous small islands, islets, and rocks separated by many inlets and channels.

When they had found the strait, the men wanted to go home. They did not care about finding the Spice Islands or anything else. Again Magellan stood firm. He insisted that they must go forward and do what they had promised to do.

One captain did not agree. Abruptly and without telling the others, the *San Antonio* turned around in the strait and returned to Spain. This was a death warrant for many of the sailors on the other ships because the *San Antonio* was the supply ship with most of the food. When they arrived in Spain, the officers on the *San Antonio* were put in prison for deserting their duty.

At the end of November 1520, the remaining sailors began to hear the sounds of an ocean. Eagerly they pushed forward, around the rocky reefs to the western entrance to the strait. On November 28, a beautiful day, they sailed into a great ocean. It seemed so calm and peaceful that Magellan named it Mar Pacifica (the Pacific Ocean), "pacific" meaning soothing or peaceable.

6

THE VAST AND MIGHTY SEA

Magellan . . . ordered them to sail through that vast and mighty sea (which I do not think had ever seen either our or anyone else's ships) in the direction whence the wind . . . generally blows.
—Letter from Maximilian of Transylvania, 1523

Sailing the Pacific Ocean was a test of endurance for the three ships and their crews. Most of Magellan's men did not survive. Less was known about the Pacific Ocean in 1520 than we know today about the farthest galaxy from Earth. Magellan thought it would take three days to reach the Spice Islands once he left the strait. His calculations were tragically off. It would be almost a year before the *Trinidad* would arrive there. Along the way were accidents, sickness, and bloody battles. Most of all, there was terrible hunger and thirst.

The three ships sailed for three months and twenty days without fresh food. The water stored in the wooden barrels on deck became putrid (rotten), and the crews couldn't drink salt water because it would kill them. Every day was a struggle to endure. After a couple of months, bodies were thrown overboard with regularity.

71

Scurvy was a terrible problem for sailors in the past. One of the oldest known nutritional disorders of humankind, it is caused by a lack of vitamin C, a nutrient found in many fresh fruits and vegetables. Since sailors spent months at sea, they rarely got the foods needed to prevent scurvy. A Scottish physician solved the problem of scurvy in the 1700s by recommending that fresh citrus fruit and lemon juice be included in the diet of seamen.

Pigafetta wrote, "We ate biscuit, which was no longer biscuit, but powder of biscuits swarming with worms, for they had eaten of good (it stank strongly of the urine of rats). We also ate some ox hides that covered the top of the mainyard to prevent the yard from chafing the shrouds . . . and often we ate sawdust from boards. Rats were sold for one-half ducat apiece, if only we could get them."

The most serious illness facing the sailors was scurvy, a vitamin deficiency that can easily be prevented with a glass of orange juice every morning. This was not an option for the sailors. The first symptoms to affect the men were swollen, sore, and bleeding gums. Their teeth loosened and fell out. Soon the men's joints and bones began to ache, and they suffered from an overall weakness. Pigafetta wrote, "The gums of both lower and upper teeth of some of our men swelled, so that they could not eat under any circumstances and therefore died . . . Twenty-five or thirty men [ached] in the arms, legs, or in another place, so that few remained well."

What saved Magellan and his officers from scurvy—although they didn't know it—was their supply of quince jelly. Just a tablespoon now and then contained enough vitamin C to keep them healthy. He probably would have shared the jelly with his men if he had known how important it was.

The ships also suffered, and the sick men had to work to keep them afloat, operating the bilge pumps for hours at a time. Shipworms attacked the wood, causing leaks that had to be caulked. Fortunately, there were few storms—the Pacific was indeed pacific for their crossing.

Fish are bountiful in the Pacific—tuna and flying fish especially—yet the sailors didn't have nets to catch them. There are hundreds of islands in the Pacific filled with game, freshwater, fruits, and vegetables. Magellan and his men came within a few miles of some of these islands, but the only ones they saw were barren and deserted.

The Pacific Ocean

The Pacific Ocean takes up one-third of the surface of Earth and is the largest of the world's oceans, twice as big as the Atlantic.

The mean depth is 14,040 feet (4,280 meters), or almost 3 miles. There are 30,000 islands of varying sizes scattered throughout the ocean. From the coast of South America to Malaysia, where Magellan was headed, is 12,000 miles, four times the mileage from New York to San Francisco. In 1521, this area was entirely uncharted.

A survivor reported that, toward the end of January, Magellan became so disgusted with Faleiro's star charts that he threw them overboard. On December 19, the sailors lost sight of the coast of South America. It wasn't until March 6, 1521, that they heard the welcome words "Land ho!" The land they found was the tiny island of Guam, one of many islands in what would later be called the Mariana Islands. (Today, Guam is a territory of the United States.)

Enthusiastic natives in outrigger canoes came out to greet the ships, appearing, as Pigafetta described them, like dolphins leaping from wave to wave. The natives clambered aboard and quickly helped themselves to everything they could carry, despite the protests of the crew. The natives even took one of the longboats, moving much faster than the weakened Europeans.

Outraged, Magellan ordered his men to fire blanks from the cannons to scare away the natives. Sufficiently frightened, the natives scurried back to shore. As a result, relations between the two peoples were damaged. When the Spaniards landed on the island later, they were met with stones and spears instead of with friendship. The armored soldiers set fire to a village of fifty houses and killed seven people. Then they helped themselves to coconuts, fruit, and freshwater.

Magellan named the place "Island of Thieves." Today, we know that the natives, the Chamorros, were not thieves but believed in sharing in a way that Europeans couldn't understand. The Chamorros assumed that they could help themselves to whatever they found because they allowed others to take whatever they wanted. They didn't understand the idea of private property.

Reinvigorated at last by freshwater, fruit, and fish, the convoy set sail again. They came to a larger island but were unable to land because coral reefs ringed the coast. The sharp coral would have torn the hulls of the ships. This was Samar, the westernmost of the Philippine Islands.

The next island going east, Suluan, had a sandy beach. Magellan ordered tents put up for the men with scurvy. He stayed aboard the *Trinidad* but went ashore every day to see how the men were doing, even giving them coconut milk to sip.

After a few days, a craft carrying natives approached the camp. Magellan welcomed them and gave them cloth, combs, mirrors, bells, and other trinkets. The men were tattooed and wore cotton skirts embroidered with silk. They brought fish, chickens, bananas, and oranges to the hungry men.

Cultural differences between the European explorers and the native peoples of the Pacific islands sometimes led to violent misunderstandings between the two groups.

Many of the sick men regained their strength, and the convoy set off again on March 22, 1521. Less than a week later, near the island of Leyte, they were approached by eight natives riding in a canoe. They were more timid than other natives, but Magellan and his slave Enrique, who could speak the natives' language, convinced them to come aboard. Incidentally, Enrique, a native of the Philippines, had at this point become perhaps the first man to circumnavigate the globe.

Their chief was Colambu. He brought them gold and ginger, both of great interest to the Europeans. Magellan told Colambu he wanted friendly and peaceful relations. Colambu insisted that they become blood brothers, which they did. Over the next few days, Magellan and Colambu forged a great friendship. This friendship, however, would bring about Magellan's death.

Spreading Christianity

March 31, 1521, was Easter Sunday on the Christian calendar. The Europeans came ashore dressed in their finest clothes. While the attentive natives watched, the Europeans conducted a solemn mass. The religious ceremony impressed Colambu, who wanted to take part. Afterward, Magellan gave Colambu a tall cross to be put on the highest point of the island. It would serve as a signal to men on other Spanish ships that they would be received as friends. In that way, Magellan claimed the Philippine Islands for Spain.

The gold jewelry that Colambu and his family wore made Magellan think of the fabled King Solomon's mines, according to a survivor's report of the expedition. Later, a Spaniard claimed that on one island there were gold nuggets the size of hazelnuts and they could be sifted from the sand. Gold was not something Magellan had considered he would find; he had thought only of spices. Perhaps the gold made him more eager to secure the islands for Spain.

Colambu told Magellan that the island of Cebu was a center for the Asian spice trade, with ships stopping from all over Asia. Magellan decided that this should be their next stop. On April 7, 1521, with banners and pennants flying, his three ships pulled into the busy port and fired a salute. Colambu's friend, Rajah Humabon, was the ruler of the island. Humabon greeted them warmly. They sat on chairs covered with red velvet and negotiated a treaty. Magellan talked to the chief and his ministers about Christianity. They seemed interested.

On April 14, 1521, a special ceremony of baptism was held in Cebu City. A large platform was built for Magellan, draped with bright tapestries and decorated with palm leaves. He dressed in a white robe—he said this showed

When Rajah Humabon converted to Christianity, he knew Magellan's army would help him gain more power over the rulers of the other islands. He was probably more interested in their guns than their Bible verses. Magellan called all the island rulers together so he could learn about the other islands and their treasures. At the same time, he wanted to convert all the native people to Christianity.

his love for those who were about to convert and become Christians. Magellan then gave a long sermon about Christianity. Afterward, about 800 natives, including Humabon and Colambu and their families, were baptized.

After the long, grueling trip with officers who mistrusted him, Magellan felt great satisfaction from the faith the natives put in him and his religion. But it made him want more. He wanted

This map of the island of Mactan illustrates the naval attack by the Spaniards that resulted in the death of Magellan.

to make everyone on all the islands Christian.

Chieftains from other islands in the Philippines were not as impressed with Magellan as Humabon and Colambu were. They refused to bring a tribute or be baptized. Rajah (king) Lapulapu was especially defiant and said he had no interest in becoming a Christian. This time Magellan's officers gave him good advice: Forget about it. Leave him alone. Humabon agreed, but Magellan refused to listen.

Most of the rajahs of the Philippine Islands cooperated with Magellan's attempts to convert them and their people to Christianity. However, one man resisted and stood against him. He was Rajah Lapulapu, the ruler of Mactan, a small island east of Cebu. Magellan believed that the native spears, broadswords, and daggers that Rajah Lapulapu and his men carried would be no match against the Spaniards' armor and muskets. Under these assumptions, Magellan led an invasion of the island of Mactan, expecting to conquer Rajah Lapulapu. However, Magellan learned that Lapulapu and his men were fierce fighters who were impossible to beat.

Magellan insisted that he would force Lapulapu to bow down. In the early morning hours of April 27, 1521, Magellan and forty-eight fighting men went ashore and attacked Lapulapu's village. The natives were ready with stones, arrows, and bamboo spears. There was a standoff for several hours, then the Spaniards ran out of ammunition. Magellan ordered a retreat. The men who were able ran for the ship, leaving Magellan unprotected. A poisoned arrow grazed his leg. Stones knocked off his helmet. He was hit with bamboo spears. Lapulapu's men surrounded Magellan, and one pushed a spear through his throat. Magellan's voyage was over.

Ferdinand Magellan discovered the Tierra del Fuego archipelago (large group of islands) when he sailed through the strait now named after him. The archipelago is the southernmost tip of South America.

7

THE EXPEDITION COMES HOME

From the time we left . . . until the present day, we had sailed 14,460 leagues, and furthermore had completed the circumnavigation of the world from east to west.
—Antonio Pigafetta, September 8, 1522

On September 6, 1522, with twenty-one hands aboard, the *Victoria* neared the mouth of the Guadalquivir River in Spain. It had been just short of three years since she had left. The only ship of the five to complete the journey around the world, she carried only seventeen of the original crew. There were also three or four Malaysians on board. The captain was Juan Sebastian de Elcano, the former master of the *Concepcíon*. He was the one who received the glory for the voyage once he returned to Spain.

The *Victoria*'s topmast had been damaged in a storm, her timbers were worm-eaten and heavy with barnacles, and her seams were leaking badly. The small crew had to keep pumping the water out just to stay afloat. A boat came out to guide them into the harbor of San Lúcar.

A witness described the sight: "On that ship, with more holes in it than a sieve, [were] 18 [Europeans], skinnier than an underfed old nag." The starving crew was fed bread, meat, fruit, and wine, and the ship was towed up the river, arriving in Seville on Monday, September 8, 1522. The crew fired their artillery in a final salute and then debarked.

As they had promised during their ordeal, those of the crew who could walk made a pilgrimage to the shrine of Nuestra Senora de la Victoria and then to the church of Santa Maria la Antigua. Barefoot, in rags, carrying candles, and weeping, they made a sad procession.

After Magellan's death, the crew's voyage back to Spain from the Philippines had been long and terrible. The rotting *Concepcion* had so few crew members that the captain ordered it burned. Portuguese forces captured the *Trinidad* and imprisoned her crew. Violent storms and malnutrition also took their toll on the crew. Nonetheless, what was left of the expedition reached the Spice Islands as promised and brought back a cargo of cloves.

The survivors were greeted eagerly in the court of King Charles V, now the emperor of western Europe. He was pleased with the treaty signed by the Moluccan rulers. It promised prosperity for Spain. Ironically, he had just married the sister of João III of Portugal and had ended the Spanish competition with that country.

Charles continued to support voyages of exploration for Spain, but most of his attention was focused on keeping the Catholic countries of Europe together—the Protestant Reformation was spreading and seemed a serious threat to the Holy Roman Empire. Some of the surviving sailors from Magellan's voyage petitioned the court years later because they still had not received their pay. No one got rich from the expedition, and several never recovered their health.

The political gain from Magellan's voyage was fairly small, although it would be long-lived. Later expeditions secured the Philippine Islands for Spain, and Spain would hold them until 1898, when the Spanish-American War freed the island from Spanish rule and made them a protectorate of the United States.

The Spice Islands were the site of skirmishes between many nations for the next century, with the Dutch finally winning. By the end of the eighteenth century, the demand for spices had decreased and the islands were no longer important to Europeans.

Spanish explorers, conquistadors (conquerors), and colonists made the South American continent solidly Spanish from Mexico to Tierra del Fuego. Brazil remained Portuguese. In the nineteenth century, all of the Latin American countries founded by Europeans became independent nations.

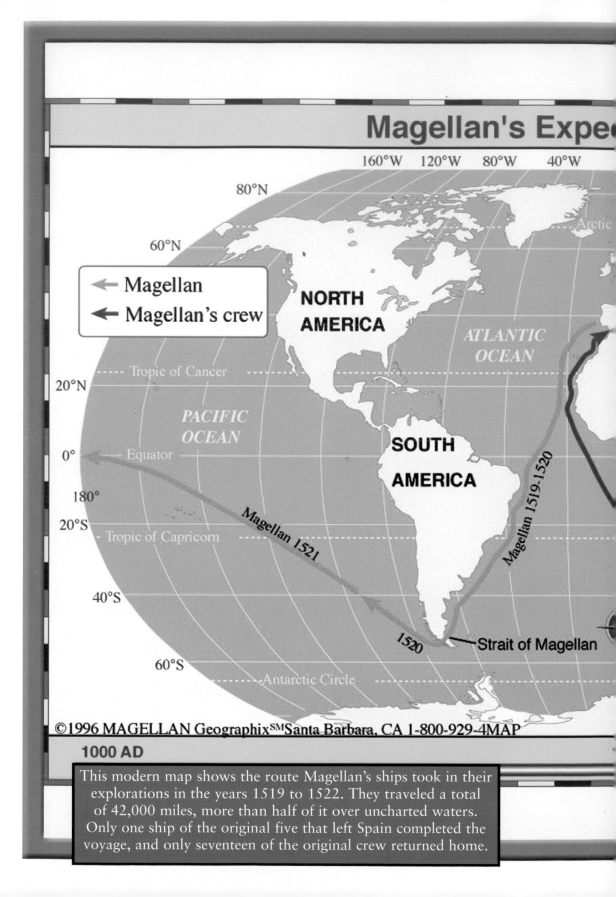

Magellan's Expe[...]

← Magellan
← Magellan's crew

160°W 120°W 80°W 40°W

80°N

60°N

NORTH AMERICA

ATLANTIC OCEAN

20°N — — Tropic of Cancer

PACIFIC OCEAN

SOUTH AMERICA

0° — Equator

180°

20°S — Tropic of Capricorn

Magellan 1521

Magellan 1519-1520

40°S

1520

Strait of Magellan

60°S

Antarctic Circle

Arctic

©1996 MAGELLAN Geographix℠Santa Barbara, CA 1-800-929-4MAP

1000 AD

This modern map shows the route Magellan's ships took in their explorations in the years 1519 to 1522. They traveled a total of 42,000 miles, more than half of it over uncharted waters. Only one ship of the original five that left Spain completed the voyage, and only seventeen of the original crew returned home.

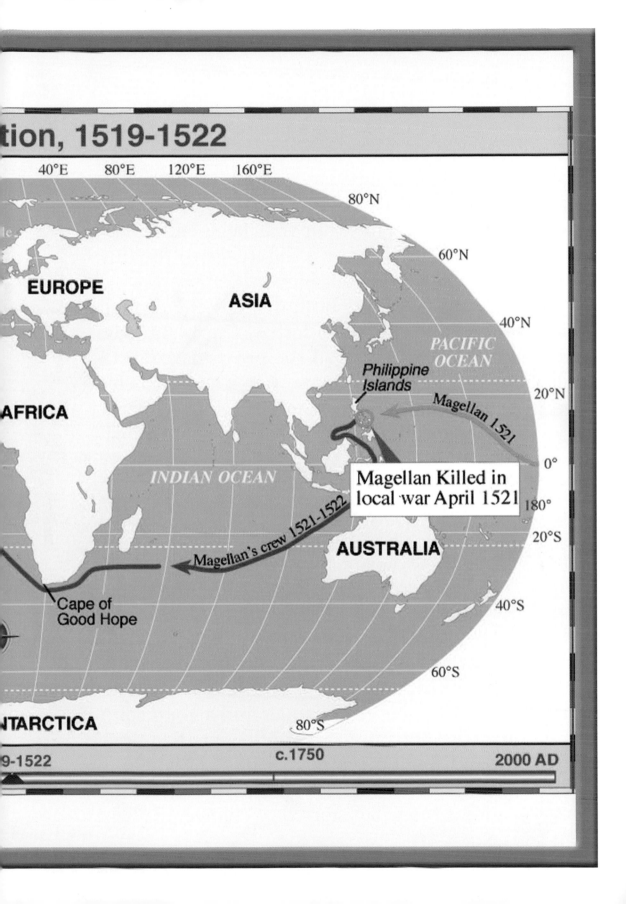

40°E 80°E 120°E 160°E

80°N

60°N

EUROPE

ASIA

40°N

PACIFIC
OCEAN

Philippine
Islands

20°N

Magellan 1521

AFRICA

0°

Magellan Killed in
local war April 1521

180°

INDIAN OCEAN

20°S

Magellan's crew 1521-1522

AUSTRALIA

Cape of
Good Hope

40°S

60°S

NTARCTICA

80°S

Magellan's Impact

By every measure in 1522, Magellan's voyage was a failure. He was blamed for the deaths of many men and for mistakes in navigation. Neither Spain nor Portugal wanted to claim him, and he was scorned by both countries. The strait that he spent so long searching for did not make a difference to the business of trade. It was all but ignored for years.

His wife and son were both dead by the time the *Victoria* returned. Beatriz's father, Diego Barbosa, made a claim for a share of the proceeds from the sale of the cargo in her name, but it was rejected. None of the family, including Magellan's brother and sister, received a penny from the venture. The merchants who invested in the voyage did receive their money back, plus a small profit after the cloves were sold.

Most of the survivors of the voyage called Magellan a tyrant and a poor commander. So did those from the *San Antonio*, which had turned back for Spain at the Strait of Magellan. Only a few people supported him. One was Antonio Pigafetta. Pigafetta traveled across Europe trying to get people to read his journal so they would understand that Magellan was an able commander and a good sailor. The diary was not published until after Pigafetta's death, and few people read it until hundreds of years later. When they did, general feelings about Magellan started to change.

A crew member who also thought Magellan was a good commander was "the Genoese pilot," the pilot of the *Trinidad*. His logbook was saved and shows that Pigafetta told the truth about the important events, such as the mutiny in Port San Julián and the concern that Magellan had for his men.

The ships themselves met tragic fates. While the *Trinidad*'s crew was being held by the Portuguese in the Spice Islands, the ship was hit by a storm and broke into pieces. The *Victoria*, the only surviving ship of the expedition, made two later voyages to Santo Domingo in the New World. Returning to Seville from the last of these voyages, she and all men on board were lost.

What Did Magellan Achieve?

Although he was a target of disrespect for years, Magellan is now ranked with Columbus as one of the prime explorers in the age of discovery. His findings changed how people everywhere thought about their world. Thanks to Magellan, people in the South Seas were introduced to Europe, and people in Europe were introduced to the islands of the Pacific.

Magellan's most important achievement is that he gave us a realistic perception of the size of Earth, its enormous seas, and the way its

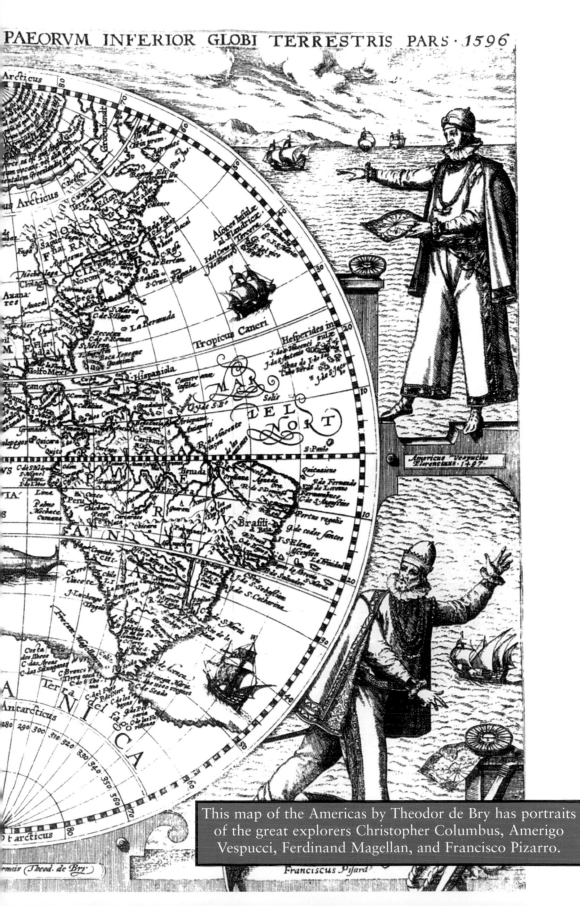

PAEORVM INFERIOR GLOBI TERRESTRIS PARS · 1596

This map of the Americas by Theodor de Bry has portraits of the great explorers Christopher Columbus, Amerigo Vespucci, Ferdinand Magellan, and Francisco Pizarro.

landmasses are distributed. This is something we take for granted today, but in 1522, it was a wonderful surprise. People had to erase their old ideas about Earth and look at it in a new way.

Magellan showed that the world's oceans are connected. This meant that world trade was possible on a scale never before imagined. This fact also proved to be very important to the world's military leaders. It spurred the building of oceangoing ships in the small countries of northern Europe and generated ideas of world conquest and great wealth. A popular saying was that whoever controlled the oceans controlled the world.

Magellan and his men gave names to hundreds of rivers, capes, islands, and mountains. In this way, they left their imprint all along their route. Reminders of the voyage can be found all along the eastern coast of South America.

Magellan's Legacy

The scientific results of Magellan's voyage were far more important than were the political or economic ones, and it is scientists who honor him today. Magellan insisted that careful records be kept of every move of the journey, with times and places recorded. Many of these logbooks and charts were lost, but enough were saved to enable scientists to reconstruct the voyage in detail.

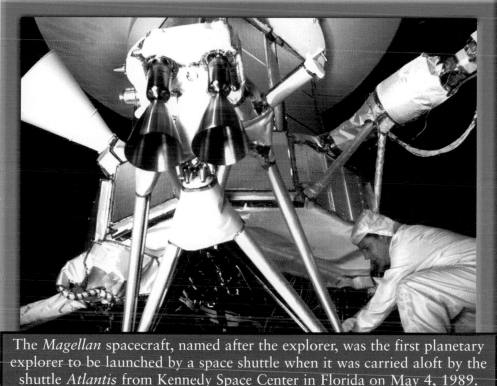

The *Magellan* spacecraft, named after the explorer, was the first planetary explorer to be launched by a space shuttle when it was carried aloft by the shuttle *Atlantis* from Kennedy Space Center in Florida on May 4, 1989. While orbiting Venus for four years, from 1990 to 1994, it made the most highly detailed map of the planet ever.

Largely as a result of Magellan's voyage, navigators and geographers perfected a system of latitude and longitude, although it would take 250 years to happen. Magellan proved that these imaginary lines are valid and that they enable travelers to know where they are and how to get where they are going, even when there are no landmarks. This led to the development of world travel in ways no one could have envisioned in 1522. Latitude and longitude also allow geographers, seismologists, and oceanographers to pinpoint oceanic disturbances and ecological problems.

Astronomers honored the explorer by naming the small galaxies that line the Milky Way Magellanic Clouds. These "clouds" are visible only in the Southern Hemisphere, and Magellan was the first European navigator to make note of them.

In 1989, the National Aeronautics and Space Administration (NASA) named the first spacecraft to map the surface of Venus *Magellan*. The space probe provided the first detailed global map of that planet. It burned up in the atmosphere of Venus in 1994.

The strait that Magellan labored to find in present-day Chile still bears his name, and near it stands the Universidad de Magellanes.

Today, in Cebu City in the Philippines, there is a monument to Magellan and a monument to Lapulapu, the chief who defeated him. Each was a hero to his own culture.

Magellan's work allowed people to see what the world really looked like for the first time. This was an achievement that can never be forgotten. Considered by most to be a failure, Magellan's journey showed us that one man's vision and determination can lead to success that can't be measured in riches.

The Lapulapu Monument on Mactan Island in the Philippines marks the site where Magellan was killed by Rajah Lapulapu, the chief who resisted Spanish colonization and forced conversion to Christianity.

CHRONOLOGY

1480   Ferdinand Magellan is born in Portugal.

1488   Bartolomeu Dias rounds the Cape of Good Hope at the southern tip of Africa.

1492   Funded by Spain, Christopher Columbus reaches the New World.

1494   Magellan serves in Lisbon as a page in the court of King João II.

1499   Vasco da Gama returns from India.

1500   Pedro Álvares Cabral explores Brazil.

1505   Magellan sails for the Indies with Dom Franciso de Almeida.

1506   Magellan is wounded in battle.

1509   Magellan is again wounded in battle.

1510   Magellan is promoted to captain in the Portuguese army.

1511   The Portuguese army captures Malacca, giving Portuguese traders access to spices.

1512   Magellan studies routes to the Spice Islands.

1513   Vasco Nuñez de Balboa sights the Pacific Ocean from a mountain in Panama.

1517   After being accused of trading with the enemy, Magellan leaves Portugal for Spain.

1518   Magellan presents his idea of finding a route to the Pacific Ocean to King Charles I of Spain.

1518   Magellan prepares five ships for a voyage to the Spice Islands.

1519   Magellan's voyage begins.

1521   Magellan is killed in the Philippine Islands.

1522   The *Victoria*, the last remaining ship in Magellan's expedition, returns to Spain after sailing around the world.

GLOSSARY

armament   A military unit and its supplies.

astrolabe   A navigational instrument that determined the altitude of the Sun.

carrack   A stout merchant ship used by the Portuguese in the fifteenth century; also called a *não*.

celestial navigation   Finding one's way using the positions of the stars as a guide.

equator   An imaginary line at 0 degrees latitude that circles the earth at its widest point.

hemisphere   One-half of the earth. The Northern Hemisphere lies north of the equator, and the Southern Hemisphere lies south of the equator.

latitude   The imaginary lines that circle the globe to the east and west, parallel to the equator.

longitude   The imaginary lines that circle the globe to the north and south, from pole to pole.

maroon   To abandon.

mutiny   To revolt against a ship's captain.

nobility   People born into high class or rank.

page   A youthful attendant to a person of rank.

scurvy   A disease caused by vitamin C deficiency that destroys the body's soft tissue, beginning with the gums. It was the scourge of sailors until the mid-eighteenth century.

seismologist   A scientist who studies earthquakes and the earth.

strait   A narrow passage, especially between two large bodies of water.

FOR MORE INFORMATION

In the United States

The Mariners' Museum
100 Museum Drive
Newport News, VA 23606
(757) 596-2222
Web site: http://www.mariner.org

Maritime Park Association
P.O. Box 470310
San Francisco, CA 94147-0310
(415) 561-6662
Web site: http://www.maritime.org

In Canada

Maritime Museum of the Atlantic
1675 Lower Water Street, 3rd Floor
Halifax, NS B3J 1S3
(902) 424-7890
Web site: http://museum.gov.ns.ca/mma/index.html

Web Sites

Due to the changing nature of Internet links, the Rosen
Publishing Group, Inc., has developed an online list of
Web sites related to the subject of this book. This site is
updated regularly. Please use this link to access the list:

http://www.rosenlinks.com/lee/fema/

FOR FURTHER READING

Burgan, Michael. *Magellan: Ferdinand Magellan and the First Trip Around the World*. Minneapolis, MN: Compass Point Books, 2002.

Fritz, Jean. *Around the World in a Hundred Years: From Henry the Navigator to Magellan*. New York: Putnam, 1994.

Gallagher, Jim. *Ferdinand Magellan and the First Voyage Around the World*. Philadelphia: Chelsea House, 2000.

Hargreave, Pat, ed. *The Pacific*. Morristown, NJ: Silver Burdette, 1981.

Kramer, Ann, and Simon Adams. *Exploration and Empire*. New York: Warwick Press, 1990.

MacDonald, Fiona. *Magellan: A Voyage Around the World*. New York: Franklin Watts, 1998.

Meltzer, Milton. *Ferdinand Magellan: First to Sail Around the World*. New York: Benchmark Books, 2001.

Rosenthal, Paul. *Where on Earth: A Geografunny Guide to the Globe*. New York: Knopf, 1992.

Tolhurst, Marilyn. *The Explorer's Handbook: How to Become an Intrepid Voyager*. New York: Dutton Children's Books, 1998.

BIBLIOGRAPHY

Collins Essential Atlas of the World. London: HarperCollins, 1999.

The Glorious Age of Exploration: The Encyclopedia of Discovery and Exploration. Garden City, NY: Doubleday, 1971.

Guillemard, F. H. H. *The Life of Ferdinand Magellan.* London: George Philip & Son, 1890.

Joyner, Tim. *Magellan.* Camden, ME.: International Marine/McGraw-Hill, 1992.

Konstam, Angus. *Historical Atlas of Exploration 1492–1600.* New York: Checkmark Books, 2000.

Morison, Samuel Eliot. *The European Discovery of America: The Southern Voyages 1492–1616.* New York: Oxford University Press, 1974.

Morton, Harry. *The Wind Commands—Sailors and Sailing Ships in the Pacific.* Middleton, CT: Wesleyan University Press, 1975.

Perry, John W. *The Story of Spices.* New York: Chemical Publishing Co., 1953.

Pigafetta, Antonio, and Theodore J. Cachey Jr., ed. *The First Voyage Around the World*. New York: Marsilio Publishers, 1995.

Schuessler, Raymond. "Magellan: The Greatest Voyager of Them All." *Sea Frontiers*, September/October, 1984.

Winchester, Simon. "After Dire Straits, an Agonizing Haul Across the Pacific." *Smithsonian Magazine,* April 1991, pp. 84–95.

INDEX

About the Author

When Betty Burnett was a girl, she lived near Long Island Sound and wondered what it would be like to sail out to the middle of the Atlantic, where there is nothing to see but water. Now she is landlocked, living in St. Louis, Missouri.

Photo Credits

Series Design

Tahara Hasan

Layout

Les Kanturek

Editor

Christine Poolos